THE HANDY LITTLE SALES BOOK FOR SCAREDY PANTS

50 Quick Tips, Deep Thoughts and Practical Steps to Selling When You're Scared

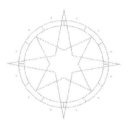

Benjamin Aaron International

BENJAMIN D. AARON

www.benjaminaaroninternational.com

DEDICATION

This book is dedicated to all the scaredy pants willing to feel the fear and do it anyway.

Sell on!

CONTENTS

ACKNOWLEDGMENTS

Thank you to all of the customers out there who have taken the time to listen to a salesperson.

INTRODUCTION

At 25, employed for minimum wage at a community garden, it dawned on me how much I hated working for other people. My boss was great, but I still hated working for him. I craved freedom, autonomy and a much bigger bank account. I was broke and needed to get out of a few bad situations and into some better ones.

So, I decided to become an entrepreneur. I quit my job, burned my bridges and leaped. I started my own business making and selling handcrafted soap and skin care products.

As entrepreneurs go, I was lit up by the idea of working for myself, establishing my own routines and not having a ceiling on the amount of money I could earn. I knew my product was good, so it felt like a goofproof way to start a new life.

Scaredy Pants

Then I realized how scared I was at even the idea of selling. I'd never held a sales job, nor did I go through any formal sales training. Okay, that isn't totally true. I did work in the shoe department at Macy's, but I didn't really sell shoes, rather I fetched them. And my training only involved how to push the buttons on the cash register and to make sure I asked the customer if they wanted to open a Macy's credit card account. Even this made me uncomfortable, so I quit after one month.

No, I came from a laboring background, working outside, usually a shovel in hand. I had no idea the complexities of a sales pitch. I had no concept of my own body language or voice tone. I knew how to talk about myself, but I wasn't very good at being courteous and attention-giving to others.

Thus, in the early stages of my startup, when picking up the phone or walking into a business to offer my products, fear enveloped me. I would get the shakes. My stomach would churn. I would blabber and sweat and spew gobbledygook, walking away not knowing what was said. My adrenal flight response kicked into high gear, so I tried to dash away as quickly as I could. My sales pitches were cragged, uncomfortable and hurried. I was so scared to sell that I almost gave up on my entrepreneurial dream before I even got started.

My fear and angst of selling stems back to my childhood. Though both my parents ended up with white-collar careers, I was raised on a goat farm in a blue-collar household in rural Missouri. Concepts around money were not talked about, and being sold to was seen as uncomfortable, pushy and manipulative. To this day, I can see the cringe on my father's face when a sales rep walks up to him in an electronics store or a furniture outlet. I learned from him that sales people are not to be trusted, and money is hard to come by, so I of course grew up avoiding sales people, sales jobs and I even avoided money, as my subconscious deemed it stressful.

But, the thought of having to go back to work using my back and not my brain was not something I was willing to entertain. As scared as I was, I wasn't going to give up. I knew I needed to learn the skill of sales before I could become a successful entrepreneur. I knew I needed to overcome my fear of selling to raise my self-esteem and self-concept.

Overcoming Fear

As much as my father hated sales situations, he has always been incredible with people, because he is kind and compassionate. I learned early in life our responsibility to love one another, thanks to my parents. As my life experiences grew and lessons were learned, I discovered a fundamental truth that has gotten me through the scariest of social situations, love.

Contrary to popular belief, courage and bravery do not overcome fear. Rather, love and kindness is the sword that pierces panic and dread. Love qualms fear in a way that eases our senses and relaxes our worried minds. Love and kindness open the door to alternative ways of conducting ourselves in the presence of others. Love shrinks the gap of separation that our ego desires.

When I started applying what I already knew to be true about love and kindness to my sales situations, my life changed forever. I applied the love and compassion I had for my friends and family to prospects and customers. I gave myself permission to show compassion to my business partners, not just my loved ones.

Love

Overcoming our fears is opening the door to more love in our life. When we learn to deeply love, care for and be [professionally] affectionate toward our prospects and clients, we will have reached a level of sales most never will.

My first sale had me over the moon. I couldn't believe it. I was in shock that I finally got to a "yes." She probably just felt sorry for me, but hey, I'll take it. After several moments of exuberant celebration, I was propelled to give it another shot, so I did. I picked up the phone and called another prospect. Then another and another. I kept trying and trying. I developed persistence, thanks to the love and kindness I gave myself permission to feel when I finally made my first sale, my first connection.

A few more days passed before I made another sale, but that was enough fuel for me to continue my pursuits. It was like chasing a high, and I was starting to get the hang of it. Don't get me wrong, it was still uncomfortable, but I was getting more comfortable with every meeting.

Selling

Like a great treasure unearthed, I discovered the most important components to making sales. I learned that selling had little to do with me or my need for validation and comfort.

Selling is about showcasing attention to those in a position to accept it. Selling is about becoming a person of service. Selling is about becoming a great listener. Selling is about becoming gentler and more vulnerable. Through the trials, tribulations and the victories of selling, I've overcome my fears and in return, I am a better person. In fact, I owe my life to the world of selling.

This Book

The quippy principles in this book aren't mind blowing, but they are useful. You see, success in sales is about having the right mindset. Without a driven and loving mindset, we will succumb to our fears, which are sparked first in thought and then in the body. Our minds will aim to fulfill the fear pattern by presenting a circumstance for us to continually be afraid. It is a never-ending, self-fulfilling prophecy of anxiety. We must understand this primitive part of our brain and supersede the fear with the only thing that it can be tamed by, love.

Even if you aren't much for the touchy-feelies, reading this book will help qualm your fears of selling because the same sales concepts in this book apply to many aspects of our lives.

Have fun with this book. Keep it around as you go about your sales day. Refer to it when you stumble, and thumb through it before your next big call or meeting. Understand that when these ethereal concepts start to sink into our mind through the written word, we pick up on the actions required to fulfill the new concepts without even consciously thinking about them.

Here's to overcoming your fears, ya scaredy pants. Now go and sell.

50 Quick Tips, Deep Thoughts and Practical Steps to
Sell When You're Scared

NUMBER ONE

HOW MAY I SERVE?

You are a servant. No matter what you are selling, you are a person of divine service to the patron of your goods. Before walking into a sales meeting or making the call, remind yourself that you are a person of marvelous service to your prospect. Shedding light on your ability to give yourself to others will qualm your fears and put you in a place of peace.

NUMBER TWO

NOTICE YOUR JUDGEMENTS

The longer you are in sales, the more often you will come across people different from you. Some prospects might be shy and have a limp handshake. Some might be overbearing and praise the politician you vehemently disagree with. Some might be much younger than you, causing you to think you are more knowledgeable, or that he won't understand your product. Some might be older and seemingly stuck in their ways, giving you the impression that it isn't worth your time.

Direct your thoughts towards seeing and understanding the divinity in your potential buyer, no matter their appearance or behavior. When we see the highest in others, even if our personalities clash, we can come to terms much easier.

NUMBER THREE

NOBODY NEEDS YOUR PRODUCT

Nobody *needs* what you are selling. In fact, there are very few needs we have as people and as consumers. If we try to market and sell our products based solely on need in a sea of options, we might be seen as too self-absorbed.

Contrary to popular edict, I recommend selling your product or service based on your message. When a company has a distinctive message, they are providing a unique choice to the consumer. The vast majority of Americans have enough money to purchase on choice rather than need, so honor them by giving them an exceptional choice.

If you sell on need, you are attempting (whether consciously or not) to engage in a subtle fear tactic, and there is already enough of that going around in our own minds to try to propagate more.

Thanks to technology, the world is becoming more transparent. When millennials, for example, are being marketed to, they fully know and understand what is happening. There are no tricks to be played. Come up with an incredible message and promote your product or service by offering it as the better choice among many, instead of a need.

NUMBER FOUR

AS YOU THINK, SO SHALL YOU BE

Think, visualize and *feel* your sales success having already occurred before you even pick up the phone.

Before a sales meeting, *know* you have made the sale. Visualize the smiles, the handshakes and notice how this makes you feel. If you are selling over the phone or via email, conjure up the situation in your mind first. Where are you making the call? How does it feel reading the email that says you've been accepted as a new vendor? How will you celebrate?

Your mind/body is an immense manifesting engine if you allow it to think and feel from the end first. But keep in mind, your mind/body will manifest your most dominant conscious and unconscious thoughts and feelings, good or bad. Your mind/body will attempt to create the circumstance to allow your strongest belief to manifest.

Thus, in solitude, clear a path in your mind to sit and imagine the joy, excitement and gratitude you will feel once your sale is made. Stay in this energy and vision. The longer you can sustain this, the more your mind/body will create the circumstances for its manifestation.

Olympic and professional athletes, dating back to tennis star Billie Jean King in the 1960s, have been using visualization to aid in their performance and success. When the best athletes from around the world started to divulge their success secrets, the learned skill of visualization became prominent in other aspects of human endeavor, namely business and entrepreneurialism.

Today, the most successful among us are visualizing their achievements before the situation manifests in physical reality. Hone this skill, and it will change your life.

NUMBER FIVE

GET SPURRED

Rejection is hard. In fact, it is one of the hardest and most uncomfortable conditions we experience as humans. Some would rather die than feel rejection.

As a salesperson, you must get used to rejection and turn it into an advantage by forcing it to move you forward quickly. When a cowboy spurs the side of his horse, it creates immediate, fleeting discomfort for the animal, incentivizing her to run faster to escape it.

For every "no" you receive, feel the immediate discomfort, like spurs to your sides, yet allow the rejection to propel you forward in much the same way a horse will quicken her pace.

Get the rejection out of the way by running faster. Always have a plan in place to pick up the phone or knock on the door of your next prospect as quickly as you receive a "no." When a potential buyer is not interested, accept the temporary pain for a moment, and allow it to spur you forward into your next call, and do so quickly. Don't wait around, don't sulk. Get on with it. When they say, "no," you say "next."

NUMBER SIX

DON'T LET THE
BASTARDS GET YOU DOWN

Ninety-nine percent of the time, it's not personal. If a prospect is not willing to purchase from you, don't take it personally. Understand that they might not be in the right place to accept your offer for a thousand different reasons, none of which have anything to do with you.

NUMBER SEVEN

10 REJECTIONS

To get over the fear of rejection, get rejected. Flip the paradigm and make it a goal to get rejected.

Do I mean blow the sales pitch? Of course not. Go about your prospecting and sales as you would any other day, but have a mental game playing on the sidelines. Get used to rejection by facing it head on and turn it into a playful experience through the most unorthodox of methods; shoot for what you are fearing.

For every day you dedicate to making phone calls, sending emails or having a face-to-face, go for a total of 10 rejections in a day. If you succeed in doing this, you are guaranteed to transform yourself into one of the most successful salespeople in the world.

NUMBER EiGHT

STOP BELIEVING

"Please turn on, please turn on, *please* turn on!!! Oh, I am a sinner, but I repent! I know I don't deserve this, but I am asking for grace! Please let the lightbulb turn on as I flip this bedroom light switch!"

Nobody does this. It would be crazy. We know the light will turn on as we walk into a dark room and flip the light switch. We don't have to *believe* in it. We don't even have to understand electricity. We just *know* the damned thing will turn on when we hit the switch.

Stop believing in yourself and instead, *know* yourself. *Know* that you are a successful salesperson. *Know* that you are getting the sale. This simple mind-pivot from believing to knowing will increase your confidence 10-fold.

NUMBER NINE

JOY & WOE

In sales, you will experience disappointment. Understand that this experience is part of what makes us human.

Don't run from anguish. As you reflect on a disappointing sales call and become disheartened, allow yourself some time to feel your woe, and understand that without this feeling, joy would not be possible. Use the disappointment to gain perspective and appreciate the challenge of what you are doing, and then get on with it (see Number Five).

NUMBER TEN

YOU ARE NOT YOUR PAST

The way things used to be, even just 30 minutes ago, is not how you have to go about things now, in this present moment.

Whether dictated by others or yourself, your past experiences, which helped you create a set of beliefs about who you think you are and what you think you are capable of, can be released if you choose.

Right now, in this present moment, you are a great salesperson. If your past does not agree, give yourself permission to detach from it. Understand that this is simply a thought you've been thinking, but the thought itself doesn't make it true.

NUMBER ELEVEN

DO NOTHING

The greatest salespeople in the world have incredible clarity of purpose.

The easiest and most transformative way to gain more clarity in your life and business is to have a moment of doing nothing. Some people refer to this as meditation. Some call it solitude, others reflection. Whatever you call it, find a quiet space and do nothing for a moment or two. Leave your phone in a different room and allow yourself to just "be" for a few moments.

As you go into silence, notice the inner waves of what is going on in your body, and contemplate feelings of gratitude, joy, love and contentment. Doing this before selling gives your mind clarity of purpose, which can allow for creativity and off-the-cuff thinking if a prospect throws something at you that you weren't expecting.

NUMBER TWELVE

FAILURE

If you receive a "no," which you will time and again, resist the notion that you are a failure, or a loser, or not good at this.

Getting rejected is a gift. It is a valuable lesson that you can learn from. Do not equate failing at a sale with being a failure. Though developing them hurts, calloused hands allow the farmer to keeping working.

NUMBER THIRTEEN

YOU ARE NOT SPECIAL

You are not special. Your neighbor is not special. The Queen of England is not special.

The idea that everyone is special is pervasive and silly. If we are all special, how can any of us be special? If all of us are extraordinary, who is left to be ordinary?

More importantly, when you make yourself special, you, by the very meaning of the concept, make someone else not special. By elevating yourself, you are deeming yourself distinct and superior to someone else.

When we reckon ourselves important or special, it sets our egos up for prideful denial and entitlement. When we are special, we don't need to grow and learn from our letdowns. When we put ourselves on this pedestal, we feel vindicated when we make a sale and slain through the heart when we don't, making it easy to blame and criticize whoever did not accept our offer, as it can't be our fault – we're special.

Understanding that we are not special is actually a *boost* to our self-esteem. Ironically, it provides us with feelings of comfort and contentment to know that we don't have to live up to the pressures of being that 'special someone' that mom and dad might have told us we are. The Queen of England gets diarrhea from time to time. She's not immune to such things. She's not special, nor are you.

Lighten the burdensome expectations you have for yourself by understanding that we're all in this together. We all suffer from time to time. We all get embarrassed. We all feel shame and remorse. We all want love. You're not special. Creative, yes. Imaginative, kindhearted and driven, yes. Special, no.

As a salesperson, don't be special. Be kind. Special is the work of the ego. We are *all* children of the Universe.

Uni = One

Verse = Song

NUMBER FOURTEEN

100% RESPONSIBILITY

The greatest salespeople are of high integrity. Having high integrity is a *byproduct* of taking 100 percent responsibility for all of life's outcomes. Releasing blame and accepting responsibility for your current circumstance—good *and* bad—is the single biggest factor to your success in sales.

Taking full responsibility for your life also provides a pain-buffer to the rejection you are sure to experience from time to time. Owning the bad with the good births positive power and control. Whatever the circumstance, take 100 percent responsibility for it.

Responsibility is the ability to respond. Hone your responding skills and release your habit of reacting.

NUMBER FIFTEEN

TRUST YOUR INTUITION

Your prospects will provide you with intuitive nudges with every single meeting, phone call or email. Somewhere in their interactions with you, through words, tone or body language, they are providing you with insight.

Listen to and feel the nudges you are receiving from your prospects and clients. And, unless you feel strongly to do so, allow your intuitive response to sit for a spell before reacting to it. Trust your gut and allow the response to form within you before reacting to anything that has been said.

NUMBER SIXTEEN

MEANS TO AN END

Successful sales = more money. More money is awesome. But, more money isn't the goal. Money is a means to an end. What is your end?

Sales become infinitely easier when your ultimate aim in achieving a sale is to provide your family with that vacation you've been talking about, or to finally pay off your mortgage, or to buy the new car you test drove last month.

Yes, it takes money to experience and obtain these desires, but if you *only* focus on the money, your desire to push through the discomfort that comes from selling won't be strong enough to push you into working as hard as you can. You need a vision. You need an end.

Allow yourself the opportunity to dream up what it is you are really wanting the money for, and then allow your desires to serve as your fuel for making the uncomfortable comfortable. Money is just a tool, a bartering agent. Your passions, not money, will always drive you to more sales.

NUMBER SEVENTEEN

ALWAYS YOU, NEVER I

Your sales pitch has nothing to do with you. Stay away from using the word, "I." Make it a game to never reference yourself at all during your meeting, unless asked a question that warrants it.

We all have the deep need to feel good. We all want to be listened to and respected. We want to feel worthy of being heard.

You have an amazing gift to give your prospects, and that is your undivided, selfless attention and respect. This gift is abundant, it never runs out. You have the opportunity to boost someone's self-esteem and even their self-identity by simply listening to them.

Make your pitch all about them and nothing to do with you. Be genuine in your questions and inquiries. Ask follow-up questions to understand them on a deeper level than the typical business surface. Refrain from talking about yourself in any capacity, whatsoever. Challenge yourself to never use the word, "I."

NUMBER EIGHTEEN

THOUGHTS ARE MIRRORS

Your self-esteem and self-worth are wrapped up in how you see yourself.

Know that when you judge others, you are really judging a deeper part of you that identifies with your judgement. Judging is a hologram.

So, if you want to be successful at sales, which requires high self-esteem and self-worth, learn to notice the judgements you have about others. Simply becoming aware of your judgements is enough to stop judging. Trying to fight away your judgements only causes more friction. Simply notice them. You can even say to yourself, "I am noticing that I am judging that person," and then just leave it at that. Over time, your judgements will cease.

NUMBER NINETEEN

LOVE YOUR PET

In sales, you will inevitably come across your PET, or Personal Emotional Trainer. This is a person you cannot stand. Know that this tyrant is here to serve you.

PETs teach us our greatest lessons. Learn to detect who a PET is when you meet one, and instead of being irritated or hurt or upset by their actions, learn to appreciate the opportunity they have given you to be more patient.

NUMBER TWENTY

STOP DOING YOUR BEST

We go through life hearing that we should always do our best. If you always did your best, that would be, by the very meaning of the concept, your normal. This would mean your best is just normal.

Being in sales is high-pressure enough. Instead of always trying to do your best, just do. Take all that silly, unneeded pressure off. Just breathe, relax, prepare and do. Don't worry about your "best." It's a silly spin on words that are completely arbitrary to whomever is judging your merit, including yourself.

NUMBER TWENTY-ONE

INTERNAL DIALOGUE

Know that whatever thought you have that is not in alignment with who you really are—your highest self—you create distance between where you are and where you want to be.

If one of your normal inner dialogues sounds something like, "I'll never be good enough," or "this isn't worth it," or "I'm not good at this," start changing your dialogue not by fighting these habituated thoughts, but by forming questions instead. For example, notice the thought, "I'll never be good enough," and recognize it for what it is. Then, ask a question, such as, "Do I really need to be good enough, or can I just be?"

Learn to challenge your old, inner-thought patterns that debilitate your spirit by simply asking questions instead of fighting them or trying to blot them out.

Over time, you will quickly recognize a debilitating thought and gently nudge it out of the way with a positive one. If you did this with every negative thought, your world would change in amazing ways.

NUMBER TWENTY-TWO

LABELS

It is easy to label a prospect as *this* type or *that* type.

Typecasting people is the ego's way of trying to separate us from a heartfelt connection that we need to make in order to have a quality business relationship. It is normal and natural for us to label people, so don't fight the urge, just notice it.

Your prospect is far too complex a person to stereotype them into a characterization. Find out who they are by asking professional and friendly questions. Remember, they want to be listened to.

NUMBER TWENTY-THREE

YOU ARE GOING TO DIE

Yep, and so is everyone you love, eventually.

So, how scary is selling, really? Is it really *that* bad? Before death and maybe even after, as you scan through your story, you will think it silly all of the fear you invested in selling.

NUMBER TWENTY-FOUR

TRUTH-TELLING

It should come as no surprise that the most successful salespeople are honest. Truth is of the highest integrity, so avoid exaggerating or changing facts for the purpose of impressing your prospect. Doing this prevents you from knowing yourself, which in turn means that your prospect won't know you either.

NUMBER TWENTY-FIVE

NAME x 3

In the course of a sales meeting, say your prospect's name a minimum of three times, and do so with a smile, even if you are on the phone. Understand that her name, the thing that tags her social identity, equipped with a positive tone, will give her comfort and feelings of affection.

NUMBER TWENTY-SIX

UNEXPECTED APPRECIATION

Call, email or show up in person to a client just to tell them how much you appreciate them. Give them a gift card to a coffee shop or send them flowers. Tell them how important they are for trusting you. Develop a sense of professional intimacy with your clients.

NUMBER TWENTY-SEVEN

WHEN A SALE GOES WRONG

Abandon the idea that it could have gone better. Yes, you can learn from the situation, but you also must know that you couldn't have done anything different under the circumstances. If you could have done something different, *you would have.*

With everything you knew to be true and understood on an emotional level at the time, you did what you knew was right and true.

So, while still gaining insight through hindsight, know that you did what you knew how to do given the circumstances. You will never improve by berating yourself over the past. Forgive any part of yourself that casts blame on anyone, including yourself.

NUMBER TWENTY-EIGHT

SEND LOVE

Before walking into a meeting, making a phone call or sending an email, in your mind's eye, see yourself providing loving energy to your prospect. Visualize them receiving your love with expressions of gratitude and joy. Relish in this vision and feeling of you providing abundance and love to your potential business partner. This will put you on a higher level of confidence and security as you make your pitch.

NUMBER TWENTY-NINE

YOUR CALLING

It is easy to get caught up in self-absorption when selling. Instead, make it your *calling*. Your calling is to be of the highest service to your clients and prospects, and make it known to your prospects your intentions, but do so from a heart space, not from the ego.

NUMBER THIRTY

INTROVERSION IS AN EXCUSE

Society has deemed introverts as shy, withdrawn or socially removed. Extroverts have been regarded as super-outgoing and loud. This typecast assumes that introverts are less successful in sales. This could not be further from the truth.

It is important to note that shyness is a *behavior*, not a personality trait, as extroverts can also be shy. Furthermore, most of the population simply falls in the middle of introversion and extroversion. The vast majority of us are ambiverts, sitting somewhere in the middle of the sliding scale that makes up our social proclivities, including salespeople.

Introverted? So what. Feel the fear and do it anyway.

NUMBER THIRTY-ONE

KEEP A JOURNAL

On paper or machine, depict what happened for each prospecting call, email or sit-down. Describe how each sales meeting went, what was discussed, how long the meeting took and ultimately what came of the situation. Even a small, spiral pocket pad that can be easily carried around will suffice, as you can quickly pull it out and debrief what just transpired.

You will be amazed how much you refer back to your journal on the precipice of a new meeting.

NUMBER THIRTY-TWO

ESTABLISH YOUR GOAL

I recommend starting with the largest goal you have, and then funneling your tangible actions into smaller goals that will ultimately reach your main goal. For example:

Main goal: On or before December 31 of this year, I have a total of 150 new clients.

150 clients / 12 months = ~12 new clients per month.
12 clients / 4 weeks = ~3 new clients per week.

Thus, all I have to do is generate 3 new clients per week. Based on this information, I will call at least 10 prospects per day, totaling at least 50 prospects for each work week.

This means that all I have to do is obtain 3 clients out of 50 prospects per week!

You see, obtaining 150 new clients sounds big. It sounds difficult. It sounds daunting. But three per week? Anybody can do that. Set your large goal and then break it down into easy, tangible actions, and then get busy.

NUMBER THIRTY-THREE

PREPARE

When you wake up and begin your day, your number one objective is to sell. Prepare the night before so that you may do so. Have your list of prospects at your workstation with little else around and get busy on your first and most important task. It only gets easier from there.

NUMBER THIRTY-FOUR

IT CAN WAIT

Unless you exclusively use email for sales correspondence, don't check it until 11:00 am Wait until noon to login to social media.

Focus.

NUMBER THIRTY-FIVE

RESPOND ASAP

After a phone call or face-to-face, immediately email a response to first thank your prospect for her time, and then set the table for the next step.

Don't linger, respond quickly.

NUMBER THIRTY-SIX

EVERYONE MATTERS

When calling a business, make sure to treat whoever answers the phone with the utmost reverence and respect. Whether or not he is part of the decision-making process, he will relay his experience to those who matter. Ask him a few genuine questions and be polite. This simple act goes miles and miles.

NUMBER THIRTY-SEVEN

LOVE YOUR COMPETITION

Never badmouth a competitor. If you are familiar with the competition and your prospect brings them up, be loving, kind and respectful to them. Compliment them as you would if they were directly in front of you.

Disrespecting your competition, even inwardly, is enough to bring about situations and circumstances for others to be critical or disrespectful of you. Dirty deeds have a peculiar boomerang effect.

NUMBER THIRTY-EIGHT

OVER-ENTHUSIASM

Exclaiming the words, "splendid!" or "fantastic!" or "bonkers!" usually doesn't sit well with prospects, as it makes you sound inauthentic. Being overly enthusiastic makes us sound nervous and fake.

Avoid sounding like a server trying too hard for a big tip.

NUMBER THIRTY-NINE

ACCOUNTABILITY PARTNER

The greatest salespeople in the world learn from great salespeople. All great achievers have mentors. Find a mentor, a coach or another qualified person to keep you accountable to what you set out to do.

This is my single biggest piece of advice in this book.

NUMBER FORTY

BODY LANGUAGE SPEAKS

One of the most overlooked manners of a sales meeting is body language. Be open and inviting with your body's tone. Never cross your arms or slouch. Hold your chin high and straighten your back. The easiest way to keep a strong, confident position is to widen your stance.

Your body language is just as communicative as your words.

NUMBER FORTY-ONE

STICK-TO-IT-IVENESS

Michael Jordan was cut from his high school basketball team. Don't give up.

Just like anything else in life, sales gets easier with time and practice.

NUMBER FORTY-TWO

BE, DO & HAVE

To be, do and have something new, you will have to do something new. And doing something—anything—is preceded by thought. Your sales success will provide you new opportunities to be, do and have, but only if you are willing to think on a higher frequency than you've ever thought before.

All of your thoughts have led you to reading these words, in this moment. Where are your future thoughts going to lead you?

Thoughts precede actions. Actions precede outcomes. What are your outcomes? You have permission to explore your outcomes now, before they have manifested, and then write them down.

NUMBER FORTY-THREE

WHY NOT YOU?

One of the biggest reasons why more striving sales people aren't doing better at their jobs and subsequently earning more money is because it never occurred to them that they could.

As strange as that sounds, consider that, contrary to popular belief, the overwhelming majority of millionaires in the U.S. came from nothing. It simply occurred to them that they could be rich, so they acted on that thought until it came to be.

They did it, why not you? What makes you so special that you can't?

NUMBER FORTY-FOUR

I AM WHAT I AM

In the world of social media, everyone is happy. Everyone is motivated. Everyone is encouraged and positive.

But we must remind ourselves that social media is a bit of a façade. Your friends and associates are not that happy all the time. Nobody is, so don't feel like you have to live up to those impossible standards.

Ironically, trying to feel good all the time actually makes us miserable. Likewise in sales, trying to be someone you are not will lead you down a dreadful emotional path, and your prospects and clients will feel your inner torment and might become uncomfortable with you.

Learning who you are not is just as important as learning who you are. Several times throughout each day, repeat, "I am what I am."

NUMBER FORTY-FIVE

ASK, ASK, ASK

Most prospects will walk their way into your sale by answering your questions. If all you do is state your set of facts and ideas without asking questions, you are leaving the door closed to any insight your prospect might otherwise provide you.

Never stop asking questions during a sales pitch. Make nearly the entirety of your pitch in the form of questions. It is even okay to deliberately write down your prospect's answers as she is talking.

NUMBER FORTY-SIX

WORK ALL THE TIME YOU WORK

According to research, in the course of eight hours of work, sales people are in front of (or on the phone with) prospects for an average of only 90 minutes.

This equates to only 19 percent of their day. Don't let this be how you conduct yourself. Work all the time you work, sell all the time you sell.

NUMBER FORTY-SEVEN

THE LAW OF PROBABILITY

If you call on twice as many prospects today as you did yesterday, your success is twice as likely.

NUMBER FORTY-EIGHT

WHEN YOU DON'T "FEEL" LIKE IT

So what. Do it anyway.

Doing something when you don't want to is the definition of a mature person who doesn't allow for excuses. Do not allow a sense of entitlement to creep into your subconscious and tell you it is okay to not work as hard as you know you can.

Our brains are designed to keep us safe, comfortable and generally in a state of seeking pleasure. Selling is none of these things, so our brains are going to give us excuses.

Notice these tendencies within you and just do it anyway. Once you start, these feelings will disperse.

NUMBER FORTY-NINE

YOU ARE DESERVING OF SUCCESS

You deserve the success you crave. Acknowledging your deservingness gets you that much closer to attaining the success you desire.

Whatever you are trying to achieve through sales (see Number Sixteen), know that you deserve it, and give yourself permission to deserve it. Guilt and shame are useless emotions, but they are strongly tied to our unwillingness to actually accept our desires. Usually the gap between where you are now and where you want to be is due to guilt and shame.

Ask yourself what is holding you back from feelings of total, unapologetic deservingness. Forgive yourself and the circumstances for whatever feelings and memories come up and change your inner dialogue to one of deservingness and excitement for what is to come.

NUMBER FIFTY

SELF-SABOTAGE

Understand that the more successful you become, the more your subconscious will attempt to sabotage your efforts. This is what we call the comfort zone.

When we breach our current zone of comfort through success, our subconscious doesn't know how to deal with this new level of achievement, so it will do everything it can to get back to what it knows. Be on the lookout for weird excuses you come up with, becoming ill or feeling guilty and shameful.

Bear in mind that your subconscious isn't trying to sabotage you because it doesn't like you, or because it is evil. Your subconscious is neutral to feelings; it merely downloads and accepts your most predominant thoughts and feelings, and when these change, it can't comprehend, so signals are sent upward to the conscious to quickly get back to what it can understand.

But the more you stay in this newfound level of success, the more comfortable your subconscious will become. Thus, this new level of success will then become your new comfort zone, to be breached again later by more success.

THANK YOU

Thank you for taking the time to read this little book. I hope it brings you comfort and gives you confidence and contentment in sales, and in life.

Remember, your thoughts and emotions largely dictate how your life is going to turn out from one day to the next. As a salesperson, you have a strangely accommodating responsibility to provide value in people's lives, and you get to do so in your own unique manner. How gratifying! Don't take it for granted. You *get* to do this.

ABOUT THE AUTHOR

At 25, Benjamin started his business path in his mother's kitchen, producing handmade soap and skin care products. His entrepreneurial efforts eventually lead him to a retail storefront and a wholesale distribution that reached both oceans and beyond. Through his own failings and successes, Benjamin developed a passion to help fellow startups develop their brand and overcome the fears that stand in the way of success.

Later, Benjamin moved on to co-founding and directing a 501(c)3 not-for-profit organization, The Lovin' Soap Project, whose mission is to empower women in developing nations with a manufacturing trade: soapmaking. The aim of the project solves two of the biggest problems in the developing world; the lack of hygiene and the lack of economic opportunity for women. Benjamin and his wife, Amanda have conducted production and business workshop training in Haiti, Uganda, Senegal, India, Tibet, Fiji, and recently had a team on the ground in Kenya.

To find out more about the project, visit www.lovinsoapproject.org.

A WORD FROM BENJAMIN

A little bit about me...

I believe in a former life I was a really great chef. Hiking and backpacking are my favorite hobbies. I love challenges and competition. I feel most alive when in the mountains. I love waking up early and reading and meditating before everyone else gets up. I can't fathom how much patience my wife, Amanda, has for taking care of our daughter the way she does.

I've recently unearthed a self-realization that I have cleverly disguised my feelings of depression, anxiety and low self-esteem through projecting the opposite. This self-discovery has changed my life, as I now understand what forgiveness (and self-forgiveness) truly is. I am more patient, kind and loving towards myself than I ever have been, and this has allowed for more contentment and meaning in my career.

My purpose and passion is to motivate compassionate people who need direction. In addition to writing books, I am a speaker, providing keynotes and leading success workshops in several states across the U.S. and beyond. I love helping people find their calling and stripping away the guilt and shame we carry around with us from a very young age. We are as free as our mind allows, yet most of us are trapped in a mental cage of our own making.

If you want to connect, you can find me at: www.benjaminaaroninternational.com to find blog posts, videos and articles about overcoming obstacles and achieving more. In addition, you can explore my private, one-on-one coaching program.

Thank you.

Benjamin D. Aaron

BENJAMIN D. AARON
www.benjaminaaroninternational.com

Made in the USA
Lexington, KY
09 September 2018